WHO DIED ON THE CROSS?

THE FINAL DAYS OF THE VICTORIOUS MESSENGER

BY FOUAD MASRI

WHO DIED ON THE CROSS?

©2016 by Fouad Masri

All rights reserved. No part of this publication may be reproduced in any form without written permission from the author. Write to:

> Fouad Masri
> P.O. Box 50986, Indianapolis, IN 46250
> www.unlockthetruth.net
> 317.410.4492

ISBN: 978-0-9962396-7-7

Layout design by Wesleyan Publishing House.
Cover art by Alesa Bahler/Legacy Design.
Production design by Niddy Griddy Design, Inc.

Scripture quotations taken from The Holy Bible, New International Version® NIV® Copyright ©1973, 1978, 1984, 2011 by Biblica, Inc.™ Used by permission. All rights reserved worldwide.

Quotations from the Qur'an are taken from The Qur'an Translation, 27th US Edition, by Abdullah Yusuf Ali (Elmhurst, NY: Tahrike Tarsile Qur'an, Inc., 2011).

Printed in the United States of America

DEDICATION

Dedication to the Messiah Jesus, the Son of Mary,
who died and rose from the dead.

ACKNOWLEDGEMENTS

I am indebted to the many people who have helped me to accomplish this project, and I appreciate their assistance. I would like to thank my editor Julia, my publisher Karen and the Book Villages team, and proofreaders Bassam, Nancy, and Betsy.

Most of all I would like to thank my wife Lisa and my children. Without their support I would not have been able to finish this timely project. I am thankful for them!

CHAPTER 1

المقدمة

INTRODUCTION

ARE CHRISTIANS DECEIVED IN TEACHING JESUS' DEATH?

A central belief in Christianity is that Jesus died on the cross to take away the sins of the world. But if Jesus was truly a prophet of God, how can he lose to men by dying?

Some imams teach that Jesus was lifted to heaven to escape his enemies, and that even today he is alive in his physical body. In this way, God was glorified, because His prophet should not lose to any man. Who died on the cross? Was it really Jesus? Or was it someone else?

The question of who died on the cross is commonly addressed with five different answers. Let's look at what the Qur'an says, what the Injeel says, and the traditional possibilities of who could have died on the cross.

CHAPTER 2

شهادة القرآن الكريم
THE QUR'ANIC WITNESS

WHAT DOES THE QUR'AN SAY?

The Qur'an talks about Jesus and the cross:

"That they said (in boast), 'We killed Christ Jesus the son of Mary, the Messenger of Allah'; but they killed him not, nor crucified him, but so it was made to appear to them and those who differ therein are full of doubts, with no (certain) knowledge, but only conjecture to follow, for of a surety they killed him not. Nay, Allah raised him up unto Himself; and Allah is Exalted in Power, Wise. And there is none of the People of the Book but must believe in Him before his death; and on the Day of Judgment He will be a witness against them."

Surah 4:157-159

The Qur'an says that Jesus was not crucified, but that those present were deceived. Who then actually died on the cross?

> "Behold! Allah said: 'O Jesus! I will take thee and raise thee to Myself and clear thee (of the falsehoods) of those who blaspheme; I will make those who follow thee superior to those who reject faith, to the Day of Resurrection: Then shall ye all return unto me, and I will judge between you of the matters wherein ye dispute.'"
>
> Quran Surah 3:55.

> "'So peace is on me the day I was born, the day that I die, and the day that I shall be raised up to life (again)!' Such (was) Jesus the son of Mary: (it is) a statement of truth, about which they (vainly) dispute."
>
> Quran Surah 19:33-34

CHAPTER 3
ظهر الحق و زهق الباطل
ISLAMIC TRADITIONS ON THE MESSIAH AND THE CROSS: JUDAS ISCARIOT

WHAT HAPPENED ON THE CROSS?

Muslim scholars have always criticized the death and resurrection of Jesus the Messiah. That is because of the verse seen in the last chapter: Surah 4:157-159. The Qur'anic verse is clear that the people who crucified Jesus were full of doubt. Many scholars interpret this verse to mean that someone else died on the cross instead of Jesus the Messiah.

The Injeel clearly says that Jesus died on the cross and rose to life on the third day – a historical fact that the Qur'an fails to mention. Throughout history, Muslim scholars have tried to defend the Qur'an by answering the question, "If Jesus did not die on the cross, then who did?" There have been five different popular theories of what could have happened, exchanged and discussed by different Muslim communities. The first four theories say that someone else took Jesus' place on the cross: either Judas Iscariot, a Jewish bystander, Peter, or a Roman soldier. The fifth theory states that Jesus was crucified on the cross, but instead of dying, Jesus merely swooned, or fainted.

DID JUDAS ISCARIOT DIE ON THE CROSS?

Judas Iscariot was a disciple of Jesus. Jesus chose Judas to be one of his disciples, even though he knew that one day Judas would betray him. Jesus had been teaching for several years and decided to go to Jerusalem to celebrate a traditional feast there with his disciples. Because his powerful teachings were undermining their power, the religious leaders of the day were looking for a way to kill Jesus.

> "But the chief priests and the Pharisees had given orders that anyone who found out where Jesus was should report it so that they might arrest him."
>
> John 11:57

When Jesus came to Jerusalem, he ate a meal at his friends' house, and while he was there a woman took a very expensive jar of perfume and poured it on his feet, which she then wiped dry with her hair. Judas complained about this, but not from the right motive:

> "But one of [Jesus'] disciples, Judas Iscariot, who was later to betray him, objected, 'Why wasn't this perfume sold and the money given to the poor? It was worth a year's wages.' He did not say this because he cared about the poor, but because he was a thief; as keeper of the money bag, he used to help himself to what was put into it."
>
> John 12:4-6

When Jesus heard what Judas said, he rebuked him in front of all the people there and told Judas to leave the woman alone. Right after this, and perhaps motivated by anger at Jesus, Judas decided to betray Jesus to the religious leaders.

> "Then one of the Twelve – the one called Judas Iscariot – went to the chief priests and asked, 'What are you willing to give me if I deliver [Jesus] over to you?' So they counted out for him thirty pieces of silver. From then on Judas watched for an opportunity to hand him over."
>
> Matthew 26:14-16

Finally, Judas was the one who led the religious leaders to capture Jesus.

> "Just as he was speaking, Judas, one of the Twelve, appeared. With him was a crowd armed with swords and clubs, sent from the chief priests, the teachers of the law, and the elders. Now the betrayer had arranged a signal with them: 'The one I kiss is the man; arrest him and lead him away under guard.' Going at once to Jesus, Judas said, 'Rabbi!' and kissed him. The men seized Jesus and arrested him."
>
> Mark 14:43-46

Judas, who had proved himself both thief and traitor, would be a very satisfying answer to the question of who died on the cross. If he were killed in Jesus' place, his betrayal would be rewarded with death – a fitting end for a traitor. Yet there is a problem: Judas's actual death is described in two different passages in the Injeel.

> "So Judas threw the money into the temple and left. Then he went away and hanged himself."
>
> Matthew 27:5

> "With the payment he received for his wickedness, Judas bought a field; there he fell headlong, his body burst open and all his intestines spilled out."
> Acts 1:18

We can see from these passages that not only did Judas die in a very final and gruesome way, he did not die on the cross; he died of hanging himself. Strangely, although Judas betrayed Jesus, he killed himself out of regret for his actions. This act of despair was recorded in the Injeel, perhaps to show that Judas did not rejoice at the thought of Jesus being crucified, but regretted it deeply.

CHAPTER 4

ظهر الحق و زهق الباطل

ISLAMIC TRADITIONS ON THE MESSIAH AND THE CROSS: A JEWISH BYSTANDER

DID A JEWISH BYSTANDER DIE ON THE CROSS?

In the story of Jesus going to the place where he was to be crucified, there is a mention of a man: Simon of Cyrene. When Jesus became too weak to carry the cross to the execution place, the Roman soldiers made Simon carry it instead.

> "As the soldiers led him away, they seized Simon from Cyrene, who was on his way in from the country, and put the cross on him and made him carry it behind Jesus."
>
> Luke 23:26

One possibility is that God confused the minds of the soldiers so that when they got to the place of execution, they crucified Simon of Cyrene instead of Jesus. However, there is no record of this, either in the Injeel or in the Qur'an. Moreover, in the Injeel it records words Jesus spoke from the cross.

> "When Jesus saw his mother there, and the disciple whom he loved standing nearby, he said to her, 'Woman, here is your son,' and to the disciple, 'Here is your mother.' From that time on, this disciple took her into his home."
>
> John 19:26, 27

These words Jesus spoke are significant for three reasons. First, the Injeel clearly says that Jesus is the one speaking, and that he was on the cross when he spoke. Second, Jesus was speaking to his mother and to a disciple whom he loved; they were close enough for him to recognize, and thus they were close enough to see that he was Jesus and not somebody else. Third, even if God had confused the minds of everyone there, why would Simon of Cyrene have worried whether Jesus' mother was being taken care of by someone? No, only Jesus would have taken the time as he was dying to ask the disciple to care for his mother.

CHAPTER 5

ظهر الحق و زهق الباطل

ISLAMIC TRADITIONS ON THE MESSIAH AND THE CROSS: PETER

DID PETER DIE ON THE CROSS?

Another traditional candidate for a substitute for Jesus on the cross is Peter. Peter was one of the disciples of Jesus, and was very close to him. When Jesus said to his disciples that they would all abandon him, Peter replied with emotion.

> "Peter insisted emphatically, 'Even if I have to die with you, I will never disown you.' And all the others said the same."
>
> Mark 14:31

Unfortunately, shortly after this Jesus was betrayed by Judas and arrested. All of his followers ran away when the soldiers took him. Jesus was then taken to where the religious leaders were holding a special night meeting to put Jesus on trial. When Jesus was on trial before the religious leaders, Peter wanted to be close and see what was happening, so he went and stood with the people outside the hall where the meeting was. But when people asked him if he was a follower of Jesus Christ, he denied it:

> "...After a little while, those standing near said to Peter, 'Surely you are one of them, for you are a Galilean.' He began to call down curses, and he swore to them, 'I don't know this man you're talking about.'"
>
> Mark 14:70, 71

How quickly Peter forgot his promise! Through the fulfillment of a prophecy Jesus had made, Peter realized his failing.

> "Immediately the rooster crowed the second time. Then Peter remembered the word Jesus had spoken to him: 'Before the rooster crows twice you will disown me three times.' And he broke down and wept."
>
> Mark 14:72

Peter's denial of Jesus is immediately followed by guilt and repentance, and he is ashamed. It would seem to follow that one who denies Jesus would choose to take his place, even unto death, to prove his loyalty. But again, just as with Judas Iscariot and Simon of Cyrene, there is no record of this happening in either the Qur'an or in the Injeel.

In fact, it is recorded in history that Peter lived, and was a major influence on spreading God's truth after the time when he would have been crucified in Jesus' place. The Injeel records his travels after the crucifixion as he told people about God's Word. Also included in the Injeel are several letters from him to various groups of people telling them how to live the right way and follow God.

Neither the Injeel nor the Qur'an record Peter's death, but other historical records from that time period do in fact say that the way Peter died was by crucifixion – but that his death took place thirty-three or thirty-four years after when he could have taken Jesus' place. In light of this very heavy weight of evidence showing that Peter was alive for years after what was to be Jesus' crucifixion, it is impossible for him to have taken Jesus' place on the cross.

CHAPTER 6

ظهر الحق و زهق الباطل

ISLAMIC TRADITIONS ON THE MESSIAH AND THE CROSS: A ROMAN SOLDIER

DID A ROMAN SOLDIER DIE ON THE CROSS?

Another person who was present at the crucifixion was a Roman soldier, not named by any document or tradition. This soldier that could have taken Jesus' place on the cross was one of the Roman soldiers who were escorting Jesus to the place of execution.

The Injeel does mention several Roman soldiers that were present at the crucifixion; some of them gambled for Jesus' clothing, and others mocked him as he hung on the cross. While it would be extremely satisfying to say that one of the oppressors – a Roman, and a person who had been ordered to kill Jesus – took Jesus' place on the cross, it is extremely unlikely. Once again, there is no record of this happening in either the Qur'an or in the Injeel; nor is there any historical record that it took place.

WHAT PROBLEM IS THERE WITH OTHERS TAKING JESUS' PLACE?

The problem with all of these people taking Jesus' place on the cross is that God would have had to change the appearance of the one who took Jesus' place. Otherwise, there are many people who would have seen that it was not Jesus – the soldiers who escorted him to the place of execution, the religious leaders who condemned him to death, not to mention Jesus' mother and disciples!

This is an unnerving theory, since it would mean that God would change anyone's appearance at any time, hiding the truth from us. There would be no way to know if the person we were talking to was actually who we thought they were. Also, and more tangibly, there is no written record of any person taking Jesus' place. Neither the Qur'an nor the Injeel teach that another person was crucified instead of Jesus.

CHAPTER 7

ظهر الحق و زهق الباطل

ISLAMIC TRADITIONS ON THE MESSIAH AND THE CROSS: JESUS SWOONED

DID JESUS JUST SWOON?

Looking at the evidence, it seems unlikely that Jesus' place on the cross was taken by anyone else. Another popular theory that should be considered is that Jesus was the person on the cross, but that he didn't actually die – he just swooned, that is, he fainted. This belief is most commonly held among the Ahmadiyah sect of Islam.

What are the implications of saying that Jesus just fainted while he was on the cross, and didn't really die? Let's examine the possibility.

In the Injeel, it is reported that Jesus was tortured before he was hung on the cross: he was whipped, beaten with a stick and fists, and stabbed in the head with a crown made of thorns.

> "Wanting to satisfy the crowd, Pilate released Barabbas to them. He had Jesus flogged, and handed him over to be crucified."
>
> Mark 15:15

> "[The soldiers] put a purple robe on [Jesus], then twisted together a crown of thorns and set it on him."
>
> Mark 15:17

> "Again and again they struck [Jesus] on the head with a staff and spit on him…"
>
> Mark 15:19

Before he was even crucified, Jesus was gravely injured. He was so weak that he couldn't even carry his cross all the way to the execution place; a man named Simon from Cyrene had to help him carry it there.

If Jesus swooned on the cross, that means he would have had to have been on the cross when he swooned, which means he was crucified.

ISLAMIC TRADITIONS ON THE MESSIAH AND THE CROSS: JESUS SWOONED

The process of crucifixion was terrible and methodical. First, the person to be crucified was laid on their back on the cross. Then the arms were stretched out and a nail was pounded through each hand into the cross. After that the feet were nailed to the cross on the bottom with the legs stretched out. Finally, the cross was lifted up into place so that the weight of the crucified person was hanging from the nailed places on their hands and feet.

If Jesus swooned on the cross, the moment of his faint would most logically happen at the moment when everyone thought he had died. If we say he swooned then, that doesn't mean that he was safe from further injury. In the Injeel it records an injury that happened after everyone thought he had died:

> "But when they came to Jesus and found that he was already dead, they did not break his legs. Instead, one of the soldiers pierced Jesus' side with a spear, bringing a sudden flow of blood and water."
>
> John 19:33, 34

So, if Jesus had only fainted, on top of being beaten severely before his crucifixion and then crucified, he received another serious injury afterward.

After this, some friends of Jesus' asked for his body so they could put him in a tomb. The day after the crucifixion was the holy day set apart for rest for them, so we could say that perhaps they were in a hurry and didn't carefully inspect his body to see if Jesus was alive or not. However, the Injeel does say that they took the time to wrap Jesus in grave clothes.

> "…Nicodemus brought a mixture of myrrh and aloes, about seventy-five pounds. Taking Jesus' body, the two of them wrapped it, with the spices, in strips of linen. This was in accordance with Jewish burial customs."
>
> John 19:39, 40

Grave clothes would be difficult to get out of; there had to be a lot of cloth to wrap seventy-five pounds of spices with the body, and the body would have to be tightly wrapped. After Jesus was wrapped in the grave clothes, he was laid in a tomb with a stone over the entrance, sealed with the governor's seal, and guarded by several men.

> "'Take a guard,' Pilate answered. 'Go, make the tomb as secure as you know how.' So they went and made the tomb secure by putting a seal on the stone and posting the guard."
>
> Matthew 27:65, 66

The swoon theory states that Jesus woke up in the coolness of the tomb and came out alive, never having died. But we need to examine the difficulties he would have faced. He would have had severe injuries received both before and after his swoon; he would have been tightly wrapped in grave clothes that were very heavy due to spices wrapped in them with him; he would have had to push away the large cover stone weighing up to two tons that blocked the entrance of the tomb; he would have had to overpower or scare away the Roman soldiers, some of the best in the world, who would have been killed for deserting their posts; and he would have had to revive and recover from his wounds on his own without food, water, or medical care, in the dark, in a possibly airtight tomb.

Although nothing is impossible, the combined weight of all these difficulties makes it seem very, very unlikely that Jesus only fainted on the cross and revived later in the tomb. The most likely situation is that Jesus actually died on the cross.

CHAPTER 8

صدق الله العظيم

LET GOD BE TRUE

IS THERE A RELIABLE RECORD OF JESUS' DEATH?

A full account of Jesus' death is recorded in four different places in the Injeel: Matthew 27:32-66; Mark 15:16-47; Luke 22:66-23:56; and John 19:1-42. All four accounts have slight differences in the details, but all agree: Jesus died on the cross and was buried, and rose from the dead.

The Story of Jesus' Death from John

"Then Pilate took Jesus and had him flogged. The soldiers twisted together a crown of thorns and put it on his head. They clothed him in a purple robe and went up to him again and again, saying,

'Hail, king of the Jews!' And they slapped him in the face.

Once more Pilate came out and said to the Jews gathered there, 'Look, I am bringing him out to you to let you know that I find no basis for a charge against him.' When Jesus came out wearing the crown of thorns and the purple robe, Pilate said to them, 'Here is the man!'

As soon as the chief priests and their officials saw him, they shouted, 'Crucify! Crucify!'

But Pilate answered, 'You take him and crucify him. As for me, I find no basis for a charge against him.'

The Jewish leaders insisted, 'We have a law, and according to that law he must die, because he claimed to be the Son of God.'

When Pilate heard this, he was even more afraid, and he went back inside the palace. 'Where do you come from?' he asked Jesus, but Jesus gave him no answer. 'Do you refuse to speak to me?' Pilate said. 'Don't you realize I have power either to free you or to crucify you?'

Jesus answered, 'You would have no power over me if it were not given to you from above. Therefore the one who handed me over to you is guilty of a greater sin.'

From then on, Pilate tried to set Jesus free,

but the Jewish leaders kept shouting, 'If you let this man go, you are no friend of Caesar. Anyone who claims to be a king opposes Caesar.'

When Pilate heard this, he brought Jesus out and sat down on the judge's seat at a place known as the Stone Pavement (which in Aramaic is Gabbatha). It was the day of Preparation of the Passover; it was about noon. 'Here is your king,' Pilate said to the Jews.

But they shouted, 'Take him away! Take him away! Crucify him!'

'Shall I crucify your king?' Pilate asked.

'We have no king but Caesar,' the chief priests answered.

Finally Pilate handed him over to them to be crucified.

So the soldiers took charge of Jesus. Carrying his own cross, he went out to the place of the Skull (which in Aramaic is called Golgotha). There they crucified him, and with him two others—one on each side and Jesus in the middle.

Pilate had a notice prepared and fastened to the cross. It read: JESUS OF NAZARETH, THE KING OF THE JEWS. Many of the Jews read this sign, for the place where Jesus was crucified was near the city, and the sign was written in Aramaic, Latin and Greek. The chief priests of the Jews protested to Pilate, 'Do not write "The King of the Jews," but that this man claimed to be king of the Jews.'

Pilate answered, 'What I have written, I have written.'

When the soldiers crucified Jesus, they took his clothes, dividing them into four shares, one for each of them, with the undergarment remaining. This garment was seamless, woven in one piece from top to bottom.

'Let's not tear it,' they said to one another. 'Let's decide by lot who will get it.' This happened that the scripture might be fulfilled that said, 'They divided my clothes among them and cast lots for my garment.' So this is what the soldiers did.

Near the cross of Jesus stood his mother, his mother's sister, Mary the wife of Clopas, and Mary Magdalene. When Jesus saw his mother there, and the disciple whom he loved standing nearby, he said to her, 'Woman, here is your son,' and to the disciple, 'Here is your mother.' From that time on, this disciple took her into his home.

Later, knowing that everything had now been finished, and so that Scripture would be fulfilled, Jesus said, 'I am thirsty.' A jar of wine vinegar was there, so they soaked a sponge in it, put the sponge on a stalk of the hyssop plant, and lifted it to Jesus' lips. When he had received the drink, Jesus said, 'It is finished.' With that, he bowed his head and gave up his spirit.

Now it was the day of Preparation, and the next day was to be a special Sabbath. Because the Jewish leaders did not want the bodies left on the crosses during the Sabbath, they asked Pilate to have the legs broken and the bodies taken down. The soldiers therefore came and broke the legs of the first man who had been crucified with Jesus, and then those of the other. But when they came to Jesus and found that he was already dead, they did not break his legs. Instead, one of the soldiers pierced Jesus' side with a spear, bringing a sudden flow of blood and water. The man who saw it has given testimony, and his testimony is true. He knows that he tells the truth, and he testifies so that you also may believe. These things happened so that the scripture would be fulfilled: 'Not one of his bones will be broken,' and, as another scripture says, 'They will look on the one they have pierced.'

Later, Joseph of Arimathea asked Pilate for the body of Jesus. Now Joseph was a disciple of Jesus, but secretly because he feared the Jewish leaders. With Pilate's permission, he came and took the body away. He was accompanied by Nicodemus, the man who earlier had visited Jesus at night. Nicodemus brought a mixture of myrrh and aloes, about seventy-five pounds. Taking Jesus' body, the two of them wrapped it, with the spices, in strips of linen. This was in accordance with Jewish burial customs. At the place where Jesus was crucified, there was a garden, and in the garden a new tomb, in which no one had ever been laid. Because it was the Jewish day of Preparation and since the tomb was nearby, they laid Jesus there."

John 19:1-42

Why would God have allowed Jesus to die on the cross? If Jesus were God's prophet, wouldn't his death in such a shameful way have reflected badly on God? One could agree, except that the story in the Injeel doesn't end with Jesus' death. There's more to the story – because in the Injeel it says that Jesus was resurrected from the dead.

Jesus Was Betrayed
"'The hour has come. Look, the Son of Man is betrayed into the hands of sinners. Rise! Let us go! Here comes my betrayer!' ...Now the betrayer had arranged a signal with them: 'The one I kiss is the man; arrest him and lead him

away under guard.' Going at once to Jesus, Judas said, 'Rabbi!' and kissed him. The men seized Jesus and arrested him."

Mark 14:41b-42, 44-46

Jesus Was Abducted
"Then Jesus said to the chief priests, the officers of the temple guard, and the elders, who had come for him, 'Am I leading a rebellion, that you have come with swords and clubs? Every day I was with you in the temple courts, and you did not lay a hand on me. But this is your hour – when darkness reigns.'"

Luke 22: 52-53

Jesus Was Falsely Accused by the Jews
"The chief priests and the whole Sanhedrin were looking for evidence against Jesus so that they could put him to death, but they did not find any. Many testified falsely against him, but their statements did not agree."

Mark 14:55-56

Jesus Was Wrongly Condemned by the Romans
"'What shall I do, then, with Jesus who is called Christ?' Pilate asked.

They all answered, 'Crucify him!'

'Why? What crime has he committed?' asked Pilate.

But they shouted all the louder, 'Crucify him!'

When Pilate saw he was getting nowhere, but that instead an uproar was starting, he took water and washed his hands in front of the crowd. 'I am innocent of this man's blood,' he said. 'It is your responsibility!'

All the people answered, 'Let his blood be on us and on our children!'"

Matthew 27:22-25

Jesus Was Whipped and Beaten

"The men who were guarding Jesus began mocking and beating him. They blindfolded him and demanded, 'Prophesy! Who hit you?' And they said many other insulting things to him."

Luke 22:63-65

Jesus Was Crucified

"When they came to the place called the Skull, there they crucified him, along with the criminals – one on his right, the other on his left. Jesus said, 'Father, forgive them, for they do not know what they are doing.' And they divided up his clothes by casting lots."

Luke 23:33-34

Jesus Died
"Jesus called out with a loud voice, 'Father, into your hands I commit my spirit.' When he had said this, he breathed his last."

Luke 23:46

Jesus Was Buried
"Going to Pilate, [Joseph] asked for Jesus' body. Then he took it down, wrapped it in linen cloth and placed it in a tomb cut in the rock, in which no one had yet been laid."

Luke 23:52-53

Jesus Rose from the Dead
"The angel said to the women, 'Do not be afraid, for I know that you are looking for Jesus, who was crucified. He is not here; he has risen, just as he said. Come and see the place where he lay. Then go quickly and tell his disciples: "He has risen from the dead and is going ahead of you into Galilee. There you will see him." Now I have told you.'"

Matthew 28:5-7

"…The men said to them, 'Why do you look for the living among the dead? He is not here; he has risen! Remember how he told you, while he was still with you in Galilee: "The Son of Man must be delivered over to the hands of sinners, be crucified and on the third day be raised again."'"

Luke 24:5b-7[1]

---

1. If you are wondering whether or not the Injeel has been corrupted, then please read *Is the Injeel Corrupted?*, another of my books. In it I examine the reliability of the Injeel.

CHAPTER 9

و لا غالب الا الله

THE CROSS AND THE GLORY OF GOD?!

WHAT GLORIFIES GOD MORE – ESCAPING DEATH OR CONQUERING DEATH?

The last possibility remaining that we have not yet examined is that Jesus did, in fact, die on the cross. The Injeel declares that Jesus was crucified, died, and rose again.

A passage in the Injeel says this:

> "I want to know Christ – yes, to know the power of his resurrection and participation in his sufferings, becoming like him in his death, and so, somehow, attaining to the resurrection from the dead."
>
> Philippians 3:10, 11

What gives more glory to God – Jesus escaping from death on the cross, or Jesus conquering death through resurrection?

The story of Jesus' resurrection is mentioned in the same four books that give an account of his death: Matthew 28:1-20, Mark 16:1-20, Luke 24:1-53, and John 20:1-21:25. The resurrection of Jesus from the dead is also talked about throughout the rest of the Injeel.

The story of the resurrection in Luke is this:

> "On the first day of the week, very early in the morning, the women took the spices they had prepared and went to the tomb. They found the stone rolled away from the tomb, but when they entered, they did not find the body of the Lord Jesus. While they were wondering about this, suddenly two men in clothes that gleamed like lightning stood beside them. In their fright the women bowed down with their faces to the ground, but the men said to them, 'Why do you look for the living among the dead? He is not here; he has risen! Remember how he told you, while he was still with you in Galilee: "The Son of Man must be delivered over to the hands of sinners, be

crucified and on the third day be raised again."'
Then they remembered his words."

Luke 24:1-8

"Now that same day two of them were going to a village called Emmaus, about seven miles from Jerusalem. They were talking with each other about everything that had happened. As they talked and discussed these things with each other, Jesus himself came up and walked along with them; but they were kept from recognizing him.

He asked them, 'What are you discussing together as you walk along?'

They stood still, their faces downcast. One of them, named Cleopas, asked him, 'Are you the only one visiting Jerusalem who does not know the things that have happened there in these days?'

'What things?' he asked.

'About Jesus of Nazareth,' they replied. 'He was a prophet, powerful in word and deed before God and all the people. The chief priests and our rulers handed him over to be sentenced to death, and they crucified him; but we had hoped that he was the one who was going to redeem Israel. And what is more, it is the third day since all this took place. In addition, some of our women amazed us. They went to the tomb early this morning but didn't find his body. They came and told us that they had seen a vision of angels, who said he was alive. Then some of our companions went to the tomb and found it just as the women had said, but they did not see Jesus.'

He said to them, 'How foolish you are, and how slow to believe all that the prophets have spoken! Did not the Messiah have to suffer these things and then enter his glory?' And beginning with Moses and all the Prophets, he explained to them what was said in the Scriptures concerning himself."

Luke 24:13-27

Jesus did not lose to men by dying; He won over death itself by His resurrection from the dead! Jesus is the only one who conquered death, sin, and Satan – to the glory of God.

"And being found in appearance as a man,
[Jesus] humbled himself
by becoming obedient to death –
even death on a cross!

Therefore God exalted him to the highest place
and gave him the name that is above every name,
that at the name of Jesus every knee should bow,
in heaven and on earth and under the earth,
and every tongue acknowledge that Jesus Christ
is Lord, to the glory of God the Father."

          Philippians 2:8-11

CHAPTER 10

تعرفون الحق و الحق يحرركم
YOUR RESPONSE TO THE GLORIOUS MESSENGER

WHAT WILL YOU CHOOSE?

Jesus died on the cross, but then conquered death and came back to life, to the glory of God. He tells us that the only way to go to heaven is to follow Him and obey His teachings. What will you choose? Will you choose to ignore His words? Or will you choose to follow Him?

> "Jews demand miraculous signs and Greeks look for wisdom, but we preach Christ crucified: a stumbling block to Jews and foolishness to Gentiles, but to those whom God has called, both Jews and Greeks, Christ the power of God and the wisdom of God. For the foolishness of God is wiser than man's wisdom, and the weakness of

God is stronger than man's strength."
>   1 Corinthians 1:22-25

Jesus offers hope to all who believe in him, including eternal life with God in heaven. In the Injeel it says,

> "If you declare with your mouth, 'Jesus is Lord,' and believe in your heart that God raised him from the dead, you will be saved. For it is with your heart that you believe and are justified, and it is with your mouth that you confess and are saved."
>
> Romans 10:9, 10

It also says,

> "If we confess our sins, he is faithful and just and will forgive us our sins and purify us from all unrighteousness."
>
> I John 1:9

If you wish to be saved, you can speak to God directly and confess your sin, and acknowledge Jesus as your Lord and Savior. If you wish, you can say something like this:

"Dear God, I have sinned, and my sin weighs heavy on me. I confess my sin, and ask for forgiveness. Jesus Christ is my Lord and Savior, and I believe in my heart that You raised him from the dead. Please be the Lord over all my life, and purify me of all unrighteousness. I commit to following You and Your commands in the Injeel, now and forever."

Jesus was the one who died on the cross, but He rose from the dead and is alive now. He offers hope and peace to all who desire it. May His peace be upon you, now and always.

APPENDIX 1

TERMS

Ahmadiyah – An Islamic sect that believes Jesus swooned on the cross, rather than dying

the Bible – a book that includes the Tawrat, Zubur, and Injeel; it is the holy book of Christianity

Christ – a Greek word meaning "the anointed one"; it is the Greek translation of the Hebrew word for "Messiah," and is one of the names of Jesus

Gabriel – one of God's angels, mentioned in both the Qur'an and the Injeel

God – the almighty creator of all that is and ever will be

gospel – a word meaning "good news"

Immanuel – literally "God with us," one of the names of Jesus

the Injeel – the Arabic name of the Gospel of Jesus, a very important book that Christians call the New Testament

Isa bin Maryam – Arabic for Jesus Son of Mary; one of the names of Jesus

Isma`il – the Arabic name for Ishmael

Jesus – An important figure in the Qur'an and the Injeel; the name means God saves; also the Savior

Jesus Christ – one of the names of Jesus; has the same meaning as Jesus the Savior or Jesus the Messiah

Joseph – husband of Mary, who was the mother of Jesus; but he was not Jesus' father

Maryam – the Arabic name for Mary, the mother of Jesus

Messiah – word meaning the "Anointed One"; also the "Savior"; one of the names of Jesus

prophet – a messenger from God

Qur'an – the holy book of Islam

Savior – one who saves others; one of the names of Jesus

Son of God – one of the names of Jesus

Son of Mary – one of the names of Jesus

Surah – a division of the Qur'an; equivalent to a chapter

the Word – one of the names of Jesus

APPENDIX 2

TRANSLATIONS OF THE BIBLE

The Injeel was originally written in Koine Greek, the language of the common people in the Roman Empire. Scholars have taken great care to translate the Bible's message into many languages so that people from all nations and backgrounds can understand it.

Some people might accuse translators of changing the meaning of the New Testament. This is very far from the truth. Committees of dedicated scholars ensure that every translation reflects the original Greek texts. Christians consider the Bible a holy book, handling it with respect and honoring the original manuscript in every translation.

In the final analysis, those who doubt the credibility of individual translations should consider studying Koine Greek in order to read the New Testament in its earliest form.

APPENDIX 2

In fact, I did that myself. I found the study of the New Testament Greek manuscripts to be fruitful, and intellectually as well as spiritually satisfying. I trust you will find it the same.

If you are wondering whether or not the Injeel has been corrupted, then please read *Is the Injeel Corrupted?*, another of my books. In it I examine the reliability of the Injeel.

APPENDIX 3

THE FIVE PILLARS OF CHRISTIANITY: WHAT EVERY CHRISTIAN BELIEVES

Did you know that Christians across the face of the earth are unified by five core beliefs? We call these the "Five Pillars of Christianity."

1. One God – Christians believe in one God.
"For even if there are so-called gods, whether in heaven or on earth… yet for us there is but one God, the Father, from whom all things came and for whom we live."

1 Corinthians 8: 5,6

2. **One Savior – Christians are redeemed by one Savior.**
"[Grace] has now been revealed through the appearing of our Savior, Christ Jesus, who has destroyed death and has brought life…"

2 Timothy 1:10

3. One Spirit – Christians are filled and empowered by one Spirit.

"But you will receive power when the Holy Spirit comes on you; and you will be my witnesses in Jerusalem, and in all Judea and Samaria, and to the ends of the earth."

Acts 1:8

4. One Message – Christians are unified by one message.

"Jesus went into Galilee, proclaiming the good news of God. 'The time has come,' he said. 'The kingdom of God is near. Repent and believe the good news!'"

Mark 1:14, 15

5. One Family – Christians are part of one family.

"There is neither Jew nor Greek, slave nor free, male nor female, for you are all one in Christ Jesus."

Galatians 3:28

APPENDIX 4

FIVE PRACTICES OF CHRISTIANS WHO ARE FOLLOWING JESUS

1. Obey the Commands of Christ

"Do not offer any part of yourself to sin as an instrument of wickedness, but rather offer yourselves to God as those who have been brought from death to life; and offer every part of yourself to him as an instrument of righteousness."
Romans 6:13

"I am the true vine, and my Father is the gardener. He cuts off every branch in me that bears no fruit, while every branch that does bear fruit he prunes so that it will be even more fruitful. You are already clean because of the word I have spoken to you. Remain in me, and I will remain in you. No branch can bear fruit by itself; it must remain in the vine. Neither can you bear fruit unless you remain in me. I am the vine; you are the branches.

If a man remains in me and I in him, he will bear much fruit; apart from me you can do nothing."

John 15:1-5

2. Pray

"Rejoice always, pray continually, give thanks in all circumstances; for this is God's will for you in Christ Jesus."

1 Thessalonians 5:16-18

"And when you pray, do not be like the hypocrites, for they love to pray standing on the street corners to be seen by men. I tell you the truth, they have received their reward in full. But when you pray, go into your room, close the door and pray to your Father, who is unseen. Then your Father, who sees what is done in secret, will reward you. And when you pray, do not keep on babbling like the pagans, for they think they will be heard because of their many words. Do not be like them, for your Father knows what you need before you ask him."

Matthew 6:5-8

3. Study the Bible

"Continue in what you have learned and have become convinced of, because who know those from whom you learned it, and how from infancy you have known the Holy Scriptures, which are able to make you wise for salvation through faith in Christ Jesus. All Scripture is God-breathed and is useful for teaching, rebuking, correcting and training in righteousness, so that the servant of God may be thoroughly equipped for every good work."

2 Timothy 3:14b-17

"Do not merely listen to the word, and so deceive yourselves. Do what it says. Anyone who listens to the word but does not do what it says is like a man who looks at his face in a mirror and, after looking at himself, goes away and immediately forgets what he looks like. But the man who looks intently into the perfect law that gives freedom, and continues to do this, not forgetting what he has heard, but doing it – he will be blessed in what he does."

James 1:22-25

4. Have Fellowship with Other Believers

"And let us consider how we may spur one another on toward love and good deeds, not giving up meeting together, as some are in the habit of doing, but encouraging one another – and all the more as you see the Day approaching."

Hebrews 10:24-25

5. Testify to Non-Believers

"[Jesus] said to them, 'Go into all the world and preach the gospel to all creation. Whoever believes and is baptized will be saved, but whoever does not believe will be condemned.'"

Mark 16:15-16

"And whatever you do, whether in word or deed, do it all in the name of the Lord Jesus, giving thanks to God the Father through him."

Colossians 3:17

BIBLIOGRAPHY

Al-deen Mahali, Jalal; al-deen al-Sayouti, Jala. Tafsir al-Jalalayen. Beirut, Lebanon; Dar al-Qalam. 1983.

Aland, Kent. The Text of the New Testament. Eerdmans; Grand Rapids, MI. 1989.

The Bible: New International Version. Biblica Inc., Colorado Springs, CO. 2011.

Farah, Caesar E. Islam (6th ed.). Hauppage, NY; Barrons Education Series. 2000.

Masri, Fouad. Is the Injeel Corrupted?. Crescent Project; Indianapolis, IN. 2006.

McDowell, Josh. The Islam Debate. Here's Life Publishers; San Bernardino, CA. 1983.

Muhammad. The Qur'an. Trans. Abdullah Yusuf Ali. Tahrike Tarsile Qur'an, Inc.: Elmhurst, NY, 2011.

Quran Explorer Inc. "Quran Explorer." 2006-2012. 16 Jan. 2013. <http://www.quranexplorer.com>

HOW CAN I GET A COPY OF THE INJEEL?

IS THE INJEEL CORRUPTED?
RESPONSE FORM

❏ I would like a copy of the Injeel. Please send me one free of charge.
   Language preference: _____
❏ Send me an in-depth study on the teachings of Jesus.
❏ I would like to follow Jesus Christ as my Savior.

Name _____

Address _____

City _____

State _____ Zip Code _____

Country _____

Phone _____

Complete form and mail to:
Crescent Project
P.O. Box 50986
Indianapolis, IN 46250

Or via email:
info@crescentproject.org

LOCK THE TRUTH

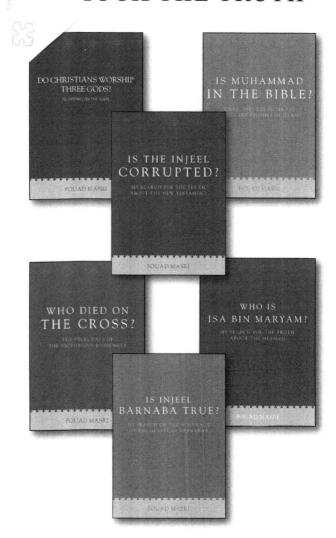

To order these resources, go to www.unlockthetruth.net.